A Night in the Gazebo

A Night in the Gazebo

Alan Brownjohn

Secker & Warburg
London

First published in England 1980 by
Martin Secker & Warburg Limited
54 Poland Street, London WIV 3DF

436 07114 2

Printed in Great Britain by
Redwood Burn Limited
Trowbridge & Esher

i.m.

D.B.
M.D.W.

Acknowledgements

Acknowledgements are due to the following, in which various of these poems (or versions of them) first appeared:

The Book of Cats (ed. Martin Booth and George MacBeth), *Boston University Journal, Dragoncards* (The Mandeville Press), *Encounter,* the Greater London Arts Association Dial-a-Poem service, *Meridian, New Poems 1975* (ed. Patricia Beer), *New Poems 1976-77* (ed. Howard Sergeant), *New Poems 1977-78* (ed. Gavin Ewart), *New Poetry 2* (ed. Patricia Beer and Kevin Crossley-Holland), *New Poetry 4* (ed. Fleur Adcock and Anthony Thwaite), *New Poetry 5* (ed. Peter Redgrove and Jon Silkin), the *New Statesman, Night Ride and Sunrise* (ed. Edward Lowbury), *Outposts, Places* (ed. Ronald Blythe), Poetry Book Society Christmas Supplements 1975 (ed. Dannie Abse), 1977 (ed. Colin Falck), 1979 (ed. Douglas Dunn), *Poetry London/Apple Magazine,* Poetry Now (Radio 3), *Thames Poetry* and the *Times Literary Supplement.*

Contents

Scare

I laughed about it afterwards,
But it frightened me at the time.

Yes;
And in entertainment, one axiom is
That scare can be terribly funny:
Those floors that tilt you
Ludicrously here, there, here
In the House of Ghosts;
The wicked fangs on the posters
Dripping hilarious red.

The real worst of horror is
Its shabbiness . . . How nice
If all private scare were awfully
Amusing to retell,
And much better still
If it really, rather wickedly,
Entertained.

— I could hoist my habitual
Skull at its fixed
Mirror in the morning, go at it
Over its shallow covering with
The razor, and receive
Such a comical thrill.

I could open its mouth, gape
Wide with it, make a sound,
And laugh about it afterwards.
It could be a real scream.

The Leap

One Xmas in the High Street, the Rotary Tree
On the traffic island by the underground Gentlemen's
Concealed a plenteous amplifier, bawling
The sound of music as if from down below.

Rotarians were shaking boxes for children
Too far away, too heathen, or too poor
To have this kind of Xmas; and two lovers
Looked out upon this scene from where they sat

— On a cushion of white noise which they could not hear —
At the cotton-wool-snow-dotted window of
A little formica restaurant, threading hands
And picking at green salads between interlacements.

That deep hum of noise from the near deep freeze
Lulled all the sounds around them, held them fast
From the clamours of the Xmas street, kept off
This world altogether, more than they would have guessed.

All they could know was a happy avenue
Stretching away in front of them, and on
Into uplands of opportunity; and they thought:
Of all the times, this time we have it right!

— When suddenly a sneaky thermostat
Cut the droning freezer out to the starkest stop;
And with a squirming chill down every back,
The whole room took a leap into a ghastly

Stillness, and vividness. Their hands disjoined,
And to their eyes came nervous, separate smiles,
Much less certain than before: that wicked cold
Went through their empty fingers to their hearts,

And froze out words. So when the shaken room
Relaxed, and as the seething copper urn
Spilled out once more its rasping twists of coffee
Into trays of passive cups, they had this instinct

Of a string having somehow snapped in the distant air
— Until the traffic moved, and the tree again
Stood and ritually glistened, and everyone
Went deaf as usual with the chime of coin.

Near Gun Hill

Once drawn to promontories where the sea
Is grey and intemperate, with sheer juts
Of rock into rapacious, upheaved waters . . .
At Hartland Point in fog a bursting roar
Blares out on time and space from the lighthouse
And deafens its own echoes; while inland
Merely a sweet haze drapes the sunset fields.
Or at Rhossilli, or the Calf of Man:
A savagery interposes on the path
Of sun- or moonlight laid across that bleak
Table of restlessness, and breaks all thought.
Once drawn to this; and therefore not believing
Any disquiet on one rare windless day
Lying down and gazing on endless sands
On this eastern coast, line above line, and each
A deepening dried yellow to the edge,
With the last line the horizon: all a stave
Still innocent of anything's notation
— And to feel suddenly how the huge chords
Don't dramatise themselves, don't flaunt themselves
In obvious frenzies here, but lie and wait
While the first creature of the swarm climbs slowly
Unsheathing a black wing and tilts one reed.

Syllabics

At a deep pool left by a high tide high on a beach,
Rather sinisterly dark green even near its edge,
And rapidly shelving away to an unknown depth,
A various, bustling, organised family
Plays happily on through an overdue summer day
At the forming of little well-fashioned knolls of sand
With the help of improvised spades hacked out of driftwood,
And the scooping of narrow, regulated channels
So that quantities of water transferred in cartons
Might be pushed and manoeuvred from one point to the next.
You can never say ants are organised while one ant
Pisses off in quiet serendipity from the ranks,
Or that humans are individual while these nine
All dispose themselves in such unison, and delight
In the antics of brackish sea water and grains of sand
Gone black with the dull consensus of the polities
To crowd out our oceans with mercantile detritus;
And you could even say that a literary eye
Was giving itself unnecessary dilemmas
In pondering whether to organise such data
Into structures of formal sense, when the thing might prove
A sociological question, a case of how
An extended middle-class family runs itself
In nineteen-seventy-eight, as it cheerfully finds
A scheme of elaborate play on a tarnished beach,
The elders pushing their young to be entrepreneurs
And learn a tremendous work-ethic learning to coax
The spillings of obstinate water to the right spot,
. . . I suppose one might let it fade, a small cameo
Of a decorative kind, quiet plastic enjoyments
Going dimmer as the figures merge with the twilight,
And the calls die distantly in the nostalgic dusk
(The parents retiring, the children turning into
Young Eurocrats, or producing some kind of let-down,
And the future arriving with its ancient, heartless,
Recurring prospect of *déjà vu* and *plus ça change*)

— Except that it glows in the mind with a feverish,
Even wilful colour, on the memory's small screen:
The cavorting torsos crazy about their rituals,
The sun blazing uncontradictably, just this once,
On a long terrain of water and sand resplendent
With an unexpected heat-wave; an erratic case
Of forgivable weather in a summer that gave
Not many days to build castles in the open air.

A Bad Cat Poem

In the spring of their hope you saw them crouching,
He outside in the sunshine and she inside,
And handling this bad cat back and forth, to and fro
Through the flap. And back through the flap.
They were trying to coax it to work the flap.

That summer the cat was not learning at all,
Though they pushed it persistently, head
First and tail last, towards each other
Through the yielding flap in the humid dark,
She inside, he outside, with fists full of moulted hairs.

And by the autumn still it had not learnt,
While the air was not kindly any more:
The flap on its hinges grated, he outside
Forcing hard the reluctant brute to her inside,
Who received it with aching hands.

It had to be winter next; it would not learn now.
It had never made it once of its own accord:
It had only ever let itself passively
Be jostled to and fro through the grinding hole,
To and fro, back and forth, she inside, he outside,

And both of them getting horribly impatient.

Art Deco Railway Advertisement

It may rain on the crags, but down in the resort
Only a sunset breeze billows and fans the grey
Nap of the boating lake into pink ripples, like
— Like scarlet ripples. Now, swiftly, she closes up
Her curtains on their small and disappearing day,
And turns with a wan smile. He sits with one hand warm
From her electric fire, and keeps the other cool
On the smooth rexine flank of her armchair. They dress
Formally, for tonight. And on the sideboard next
The window, on her right, stands a neat cut-glass pair
Of sweet aperitifs. He will not look her way,
But focuses the ashtray on its leather strap,
Where she may lately have set down her cigarette:
Nothing has yet deranged its drawn-up thread of smoke.
Whatever they may do when dusk has turned to dark
Is hidden from us yet (was hidden from us then)
So all we might conjecture from their perfect poise
Is that the most she feels concerning his profound
Conviction of her cold, impermeable grace
Is a sympathetic spiritual regard;
And envying their world of carefully-defined
Limits and chances (they need never travel on
To places where correct patterns of gesture make
No real impression on the bloody flux of things),
I can see reasons why, some forty years ago,
The self I am today should 'Spend a Day in Hove'.

In Praise of Nostalgia

Condemn it as a *fainéant* indulgence;
But nations without it fix their constitutions,
Buy personnel carriers from Western powers,
        And refine kinetic art.

Having nostalgia is having a proper respect
For small lights receding on a shore, without
Dismissing *all* pioneers who sternly steam off
        Across the Forward Planner.

Not having it is licensing Zakki and Tobia
To patronise Nik and Germaine for their funny names
In 1998. Is saying, 'Look at these craptious
        Gears in these merdy old photes!'

When it's not as if the nostalgic were saying
'Revere them in their dignified garments, fragile
In the beautiful black-and-white past; from them
        We derive all truth.' We are not such fools.

One bad mistake, I agree, is reducing nostalgia
To wanton revivals of old detritus:
Hobbit socks and Whitelaw cardigans need not
        Come back again in my lifetime;

And one better form of nostalgia is a hatred
Of the arrogance of time ever passing: Adolf Hitler
Drank gallons of weak tea and ate cream cakes,
        And raved all night about the *future*;

He should have sat with the nostalgic, reminiscing
From evening round to dawn, and when dawn comes
One says, 'Do you remember how we sat last night
        Indulging our nostalgia? How sweet it was . . . '

Then didn't someone say nostalgia was not
A weakness, but a springboard? From where you stand,
With the warm past cheering you on, you dive away
          Into the coming minutes reassured

That they also will cheer you to recall them.
Don't listen to any injunction to 'Cut adrift,
Forget what you cannot change.' Think long enough
          About anything past, and it improves.

— My horror is of losing all regard for any
Caress, or meal, or music from yesterday. I would never
Willingly let it all go slipping like a splendid
          Orchestra out to sea. My dread

Is of being a forgetful old man at ninety
Hustled onwards, always onwards, turned right off
The dances of his youth (though he rarely danced them)
          And set there, stark upon the shore,

Amidst a rubbish from times-to-come: the trees
Casting polythene leaves, the calendar metric,
And each bit of flotsam swirling round his feet
          Singing, 'Hey! My name's *Tomorrow*! Bite me
                                        NOW!'

Chiefly Learned in Courtesy

You may leave the lift first, I will stand and keep
Its butting doors apart, and let you go.
Your smile is the pleasure of being flattered
With tiny politenesses, nothing in the least
Flirtatious in it. Why should there be that?

In me, I feel today my ancient daring
Neutered into disgusting gallantries
. . . Risible old Ruritanian courtesies:
A tubby Rassendyll, approaching sixty,
Scraping around in the ends of emptied eggs.

Representational

His mother's wrinkled gloves have been warm enough
For the glass of the table where they lie to steam a bit:
These three are sat on gold-painted cane armchairs
In the middle of a spa, the man quite readily benign,
And smiling at the seven-year-old boy, though he hasn't
Much to say, and he sucks a thin cigar.
                                                            A lady
In a purple topcoat leaves the counter and brings,
On a green tray, coffees and orangeade, she glides
Into their circle deftly with a quiet, adaptable
Smiling. This December is cold, but the sweet
Orangeade shrills heavenly up the waxy straw, a cool
Perfect runnel over his tongue, it's 1974.
                                                        His mother
Is flushed and laughing with the man, there they are
In the great wall-mirror on the far side of the room,
Laughing and flushed the two of them, the freer selves
They could always be if this were only art
— Oh, if this were only art, or even fiction! But still,
Small rewards and mercies hold good . . .
                                                    And the little boy
Now draining the last sacramental droplets from the glass
Quite likes the man, and the sun is coming out.
The lady with her emptied tray makes an adult smile
For the adults, and a children's smile for the child;
Her petition forms on the counter, to which she returns,
Are nearly filled, so the Ring Road is nearly prevented.
                                                            The man
Will have paid off the Datsun in just under five months' time.

The Information

When the Library of Congress is finally
Reducible to a cube one inch by one
Inch by one inch, you are going to need to lose
Absolutely nothing: stored and retrievable

A pear-core once left gangling on an ashtray,
The moment of Amanda's purple scarves touched
Sadly into order, the whole of *Le Figaro*,
And the accurate timbre of all your departed
Cryings-in-the-night. None of this
Will be vanishing any more.

Up there, instead of shining empty sky
(The still clear sunlight you are walking in
With terrors in your head) will be
A building specially built to set this right:

In any of a thousand rooms it will
Be possible for somebody to remain
For all of life after infancy till death,
Fed and evacuated and re-clothed
In a see-through cubicle, flicking up fact after
Fact and image upon image, actually
Playing his infancy back; working with his keepers
At the reasons, there, for needing to do such a thing.

Point of Honour

On a wet South Coast night when even
Believers in rain and luxuriance are resenting
How drenched the leaves are on the trees outside
Their pelted windows, a dark-haired girl lies lamenting
How far love seems from any dreamed-of heaven
— As this egotist who has just straddled her, and cried,

And slumped into a heavy shagged-out quiet,
Says, reaching for a well-placed cigarette,
'If I'm hurting your right leg, dear, please let me know.'
And oh, it is her *left* leg which he needs to get
Clear of to reach the matches; having come to lie at
A clumsy angle during his last, slow,

Gratifying turmoil, which has nonetheless
Been too fast for the girl by half.
                                        Now she has heard
Sam. Johnson's words, 'To scratch where there is an itch
Is life's greatest pleasure.' And she forgives her absurd
Seducer's selfish haste. And she feels worse distress
That he thinks it her *right* leg on his right side of the bed

— Since a gentleman could tell which limb was which.

At Middleton St George

The buzz of a mechanical game played by working
Two handles, one on each side of a screen
Where you shift around an always-too-late white line
In the effort to stop a blip which flies very fast
Over a small dark firmament, you lose a point
If you don't contrive to intercept it; and gin,
And bubbles rising in the tonic, or clinging
To the side of the glass, expiring hopes:
An aerodrome building, converted not long back
Into a student lounge, with bar and cushions,
Double-glazed against the whining air, but somehow
The room is forced to admit the scream as it pierces
The level land outside, jet engines droning
On their high and undismissible register, dropping
Down fast to this haven of their firmament,
A sound striking suddenly through, as when you feel water
Reach inside a soaped ear.
                The runways were laid down
For a war predating mechanical games you can play
On buzzing screens, but resulting in radar,
And out across the acres of grass and tarmac
Stand air-force buildings of one and two storeys
Converted into a college for several hundred,
Made over into bedsits and lecture-rooms and that
Barrack is the library, with long open aisles
Of volumes for learning about learning.
                        Sitting there
You can try intercepting an idea before it flicks past
(Without working a handle) but not for long now:
The engines will soon inherit the place again, the ideas
Expire, like all hopeful bubbles. For thirteen years
You could eat in the echoing refectory, run
A moderate lap on the games floor laid down inside
The hangar; but an unlettered wind wipes all
This land quite clean of learning, the students leave,
The last ministrants see them out.
                    Eight years ago,

Ruth furrowed in that index for critical assistance
With the novels of D.H.Lawrence, and walked along
To a corner where they went to each other's arms
And her shoulder, for a moment, unbalanced a small row
Of volumes at 823.LAWR. And eight years ago,
They all fell back into place, in perfect order,
As he let Ruth go, not to be kissed again ever
By him, and watched her recede down the heartless
Perspective of the grass, farther off and farther still,
And go in for her Finals.

                     The ceiling of chandeliers
Above our student lounge makes a carapace against
The huge skies of this region, but the crude lid-lifters
Will prise it away, and we shall shiver
From more than nostalgia, and then relinquish it
To the fractured sky over the runways, allow
The Lawrence files to break open at their spines, pages
Flutter away into the slipstreams and vanish
In a distance which does not read. The flying blips
Fled past too fast, we were always too late.

                             That ivy,
Which grew untrained up the wall of the Admin. block,
Rattles red against the brickwork, the colour it turned to
And stayed throughout last winter, a louder sound
Than any inside, where the rooms now scream with silence;
And there's the last bubble faintly expiring in
Our tonic water, like a lamp of Europe.

                           Oh, but now
There is suddenly a triumphant jumping of feet
On the carpet up by the screen, because someone
Has deflected his final blip, and won! What a pity
It's a game and not real . . . One says about the real,
There are too many evils to prevent, or even
Notice them all, as you strive to work the hopeless
Handles you are offered, like using sardine-tin keys
For programming computers.

                       There was Ruth here once,

And the fall of her hair across the shaken spines
Of the Lawrence critics, and her lover's spine tilting
Towards her at 823.LAWR. He was one who read,
Like most of us, not wisely but too late,
And what should he have learnt?

                                And what have I?
— Hardly much more than one negative consolation:
There are too many evils, they race too fast, you lose
Much more than a point if you don't contrive to intercept
                                           them.

We Try

> Music runs in our family,
> Music runs right down the generations

I take out the Banjo Tutor from the stool:
Unthumbed after seven pages

. . . That sound in the next room when we visited
Was my girl cousin, vamping by herself

> Music runs in our family,
> Music runs right down the generations

Our tree nested so many singing birds:
Grand ballads done to little uprights

My uncle burnished a harmonica on his sleeve,
He was trying to get it to his mouth

> Music runs in our family,
> Runs right down the generations

Our bosom aunt and the man with the tympani,
And many a good tune played on an old

— And here is a hidden photo of the Black Sheep
Taken posing with a cello

> Yes, music runs in our family,
> Runs right down the generations

All this was before recorders, and down
Market from madrigals

It was all worth the trying, but it fell away
From our lives and our deaths like discarded scales

But music runs in our family,
It definitely runs in the blood

And as for me, I plug
The organ in, switch on, and run one hand

Heptonstall February

Today the moors unclench and clench
On a gift of warmth; the snow
Draws back one softened inch, but frost holds firm.
In our mid-afternoon new ice already
Glints, in the sun's very eye. A camera-eye
Would trace the loosened stream, and stop
On a rigid freeze: where suddenly grey
Spires, that were a waterfall, stab down
At the shrunken torrent.
                             None of these days
Will release themselves, the land
Not gentle into sympathy. This cold
Is well ignored by those who wait indoors
Inside their coloured windows, watching
The month increase and the land not change:
Let it come to the light and listen.

Afternoon in the Fens

Then the farms ended, and the last dyke
Gave onto reeds, to mudlands; beyond which
A lightship blinked in the haze where the mud became the
                                                    sea,
And that afternoon, two black and circling specks
Droned like gnats in that distance beyond our reach.

A dubious peace, the water shrunk down in the channels
Under clumps of bleached, unstirring grass;
A drugged end to August, the dyke-track
Dusty under four people's shoes where we stopped,
Gazing at a high square of wood braced

On a frame of iron in one field-corner. — And suddenly,
Out of the faint waters, the two droning dots
Enlarged towards us, two furies homing at this
Target we were standing near on the dyke, coming
Each ninety seconds and screaming and screaming

At the square of orange-painted slats clamped
On black poles of iron rusting into the rich earth,
Laying down fume trails onto smoke from the
Straw-fires left by farmers affluent on
Their steady reclamations of mud.

After two screamings our hands held our ears
As we moved aside along the narrow path,
But the two planes turning again over the flats
Avoided the target, were diving at, screaming at
Us, furrowing the air with billowing smoke-lines,

Homing at the four of us walking this bank
Between farms and land-finish. Out on the far sea
The lightship blinked to no one in the shallows,
And no one elsewhere moved in the fields
Under a sky impenetrably clear, curiously

Dulled by the heat-mists. Again and again,
Turning and screaming ancient, reasonless
Hatreds, they followed; then finally wheeled away, back,
Out over the sea, where the lightship continued to warn
Among sandbanks stuck with wrecks from recalled wars.

Dea ex machina

The woman with legs long for her family,
And the man with short legs, a short-legged man,
Match perfectly in the kitchen before Anna comes:
Anna, after a decade, at the wrong moment, back.

The crockery is streaked, and rattled dry,
And will have to be re-washed better by hand.
'Start over!' Anna will say, being American,
And they will have to unmatch their thighs, which
Will be aching, and may be slightly shaking,
And wipe at least forks to make a snack for Anna, back
Oh God, on the scene after ten years gone and not regretted.

It took no little time for these two to match,
For each to find the words, and their legs to lodge
One against the other and the other one
Against the other one, respectively,
In a sort-of logical comfort.
                                        So may not
The telephone, vicious in voice or in silence,
Or the neighbour, preening her jubilee rosette,
Or finally Anna returning, any second now
— An emanation from her own dishwasher, all
Streaked with happy tears — break
This decent duo up.

The World Outside

When poetry was a landscape art, arranging
Syllables in a noble sweep to gaze up, the vista
Was the big house of order and seclusion, stately
Between stiffly regular lines of most proper trees.
The world kept out was the goatherds and their pipes.

When *civitas* seemed quite possible, the view
Was the city square, across a purified *parole*
— Incredibly kempt, and engraved with some token bourgeois
Respectably strolling out. Small in the foreground, the rest of
                                                        the world
Was the mongrel dog that whined at the flawless space.

Seeing the lift 'Out of Order' he mounts the stairs
Helped up by a loosening banister, and sees
Poetry striving to root in a tub of dying plants
Put down on a vinyl landing. The poor pale thing
Is hungry for sense and sanity, wincing at

The sight from this fifth floor window, and craving
Simply to understand: four lanes of a freeway
Mesh with six lanes of another below him, and the sun
Amazedly glitters off the flank of twenty-two
Office-floors across the street. At the ninth landing,

He knows that this world won't be excluded. It goes with him
Into a room where fifty are gathered together,
All drinking to efface the scenery. Traffic management,
Retrieval systems, God, can't contain this world;
So words will somehow have to.
                                        'Hullo,' he says,

'I've read your book, I think it's really great.'

Especially

To Frank and Rita in Bracknell, greetings,
And greetings especially to those listeners who,
On this weatherless February day at half-past four,
Have risen from first long lovebeds in small warm rooms
To lie again in magenta baths together,
And dabble each other's steaming thighs with suds.

I especially feel
For those who have long-delayed essays on Tennyson to write,
And have switched on their English transistors to discover
Some Third Republic operetta tripping out
On Radio 3, all coquettish plaints
And cavalier manoeuvres, happening out there
In the distance and the past, and so near and true.

May you, especially, recline, as you listen to the voices
Of love made easy and gracious ploys fulfilled,
And renew the heat of the water from time to time
From the tap marked 'Varm' (if you're listening in
                                                    Stockholm),
And float the soap in play towards each other's
Crotches, in the softly dropping dark,
And chatter for only a sentence or two of what
Might be, and what might prevent it in a thoughtless world.

Greetings to you then, especially, and here
Is *Das Lied von der Erde*.

A Night in the Gazebo

I

Look down into hotels where girls work
                In their vacations,
And in the early evening, managers, averaging
Forty-six years old, induce them to upper bedrooms,
Empty because business is dropping off:
Think of the protestations round the coasts of England,
The moaning on the candlewick coverlets,
And the girls so young, this the first time for most of
                                                    them,
And the managers cautious and honourable,
Saying they won't go too far, and going
Too far, the girls done with A levels,
And the managers pressing and leering and the minds blown
                                                    for days.

II

Look down at one manager at seven-thirty, all his girls
                Heltering through his mind,
And fewer girls each year in the last three years,
But this year more girls than for three years past,
Five girls to be exact, so it is spring once more
And the blood sparkles, at an average age
Of forty-six. There he is now, leering in the glass
Behind the lounge bar, tilting, adroitly, Chartreuse,
Thinking of his five girls this season: Tina, Prue,
And Elaine, and Kirsten, who pulled the scarlet
Curtains herself, and Rosemary, queen of impermeable
Silence, who will come back of her own accord.

III

      Look down there at the window of a room at dusk
             Where a pensive manager,
Letting the twilight change to dark, sits alone
Without a light at nine-thirty, run out of cigarettes,
Sits alone, eyes open, in a crumbling swivel chair.
Now he hears the feeble whine of a slow lift,
And a girl comes in who understands his sadness,
Business declining and years declining
— And a good love quickens in this very young girl,
Or a love upgraded from pity (she has brought some
                                    cigarettes)
      For a manager pining heavily in a hotel
Not doing particularly well . . .

IV

      Look down at a boy friend emptying fruit machines
             On the pier at ten-fifteen,
After a fair day's business. The ogling machines
Are adjusted finely to concede just a little
And grasp the rest to themselves,
And his girl is adjusted finely in the same way
— Because of a manager of a hotel (where they
Spend the early evenings in an upper bedroom).
She is meeting the boy in the Bull, and
For him life feels like a nasty row
Of mocking variables, apples, plums and flags,
As he filches the coins with which he will buy the drinks.

V

And look at this boy friend at midnight
      At the girl's gate:
Now cradling the sobbing girl, who has told him
Everything all at once in a sudden gush.
She says she could be sick, which she could not,
And the boy is sick instead because it has taken
Eleven pale ales to her four bacardis-and-coke
To bring her to this point of revelation.
Thus: the manager, his girl friend, and her boy friend —
It's a bad time for all of them (though at this moment a
                                    letter
Is on its way to the girl to say she has
Two D's and an E and a place at the North-East Polytechnic).

VI

But look again at this boy friend, who is feeling better
      Up the hill past the Cats' Home
On his long walk back about an hour later.
He is compassionating the manager in question,
Whose letters he has been shown: 'Dear Tina,
I long for you all the time . . .' and similar things.
He can guess the timeless agony of the man,
Longing so much for the girl he more or less
Longs for himself, and he is not so jealous.
He could be in the same position one day.
He could be in the same . . . He is overcome
With a selfless presagement of the nastiness of time.

VII

Look between the chink in the curtains
    In one hotel window,
Where a manager, at one-thirty, is turning a coverlet
Down, the only coverlet he ever turns
Down, to slink into bed beside his wife.
Groping the pillow in the darkness, this manager
Thinks of that day's baffling girl: 'You've never
Read any Gary Snyder or Frantz Fanon, you've hardly
Heard of Claes Oldenburg or Roland Barthes,
Or of Simon or Garfunkel,' she had said in reproach.
'Do you call that living?' — 'Yes,' he thinks,
As he thinks of her left breast flipping the back of his knee.

VIII

In the terrible small hours look over
    Everyone fitfully asleep,
And do not imagine they do not have complex dreams.
E.g., a girl is at the bottom of a slimy pit
With smooth sides, and hairy managers are toppling
Hairy managers in rockers' goggles down on her,
So that she screams; only the scream
Comes out a bit ecstatically and she can't
Explain to herself why this should be really so,
Or how she should have come to be here at all.
It stays with her while she dresses for another
Long day at the hotel. She can't wait for the early evening to
                              come round.

IX

Look into a corridor where a girl at nine-twenty a.m.
       Walks carrying sheets,
And a second follows, to shake them out with her,
One girl moderately appealing and the other
Less appealing than her, not least in her perceptions
(Which she keeps to herself). The conversation
Is equivocal, since they are discussing the manager
And the first girl has more to disclose than she says,
Though she is hinting, continually hinting,
In the faint breeze from the sheets. Small tabs with
Laundry numbers fall off the outflung linen,
And the bedroom radio sings of *'leurs déguisements*
                        fantasques'.

X

Lastly, gaze out there at the crematorium.
        Having consumed fourteen
Tequilas in half-an-hour, a manager
Is being consumed to rest. His wife comes first,
And behind her follow forty-six girls in all,
The youngest sixteen, the oldest thirty-four,
And all in states of nostalgia or raw distress
According to how lately they knew the man.
So wife and girls compassionate each other
As the clergyman, noting an ancient English
Ritual of mourning, shakes each girl by the hand.
If this can happen, the world must be good. It is ten forty-
                        five.

Lost and Found

The knights on his first chess set were mounted
On horses with close-together eyes and narrow noses:
An amused look whichever way they faced.
One day, the set was not complete. A knight
Was lost, he played half-heartedly for thirty years
With a plastic pepperpot instead. She walked into his room
Eventually at forty-one, with a set smile
And amused eyes close together under her forehead.
She took a step, and turned aside, smiling.
Consequently life could be played properly again.

The Dolls' House

Sixteen miles from anywhere larger
On the map of a renamed county,
With an ancient market-square to which
Sore-faced farmers drive flocks in brown, tiered
Lorries every Thursday, is this
Country-town: a pestle-and-mortar
Restaurant, a glinting pharmacy
With rows of touched-up tincture jars, a
Salon of 'Gowns', one minimarket
Grocery, and a furniture shop.

Past the last black-and-white traffic sign,
The last lights in small manor-houses
Go out, and one more squirearchical
Day is done with; county magazines
Lie smoothly on their own in the dark,
The warm engines of the GL-12s
Click and settle in their garages
In villages where old bachelor
Campanologists tire, and hunger
At last, leave their ropes and sprint off home.

Through the glass of the furniture shop
A sleek room gleams, indescribably
Tidy and perfect: purple wall lights
Allure and chill, and a magenta
Carpet sets a table and two chairs
Fast in the specific attention
Of two poised lamps. This is a ghosts' room:
Two especially, two spectrally
Immaculate-feeling people could
Stop and repose here at two a.m.

As exactly pure exemplars of
How things ought to be. It would give them
That virgin bed with a canopy
In the background, spaced silken pillows
Asking those who have walked at a fixed
Distance for so long to lie, chastely
Apart, until the first unpolluted bird
Announces dawn. Shall we step inside?
I can't think we or it will ever
Suit each other quite so well again.

Night and Sunrise

The cog-wheel abrasions are at it again
On this first glinting day of March,
Swerving over any pale surface, fastening
Blips of a crazed illumination on
The walls, the carpet, the half-typed page.

So again the old half-humorous yearning starts,
For the life of the darkest months:
The sunless heavens, the velvet hours
When action soothes, and shadow into shadow
Glides for a shadow-satisfaction.

— And truly, the heart of the educationist
Rises in autumn, as dead leaves drift
Round blocks of switched-on light in heated rooms;
The colours of that season moderate
The strident freshness on those shoots of green . . .

Reproached one late June day, when she maintained,
'Dark nights, cold weather, cold women,
Those are what you seem to want!' I tried to say,
'Exegesis is so difficult in summer,
My eyes can't tell the words from the spaces

In a book read out of doors. Besides,
Your sunshine only lights the surfaces,
And deep down things the dearest darkness lives,
Where profundity waits to be dug for'
— When she put the book aside, and we went indoors

Discussing my eyesight and my character,
Regretful or happy that the nights were already
Drawing in, and she closed the curtains.
                                                    Who had won
I could not tell. We let things rest between
The dark and light . . . But I was glad she stayed

To try the night, and see the dawn up for me.

An Elegy on Mademoiselle Claudette

Mourning the final death from disbelief of one
Who lies now farther out than her rival's sword;
The sea, having had her at last, being
A fit receptacle and outcome. She
Was thirty-two when she died, I having
Given her first credulity when I was eight,

And the ideal reader. Somewhere they met,
Her fatalism, my childhood, and made strange friends:
She held her world with fingertips of ice
On chalices of poison. She was in the eyes
Pulling mine at fifteen over café floors, she stared
Out from trains, she dared in time to come near and be

No different, even when she undressed. The spell didn't
Break, because she was always gone next morning,
A skyline figure on horseback, not leaving a note.
And this continued some while, her cloak
Flowed at numberless parties, and she nurtured
Linguistic codes beyond mine, and had flats

(Which I never went to) all mauve lights and white divans,
Acting indestructible enough to be
A life-force in her way, a fuel for one kind
Of imagination. But what could she keep when
Life coarsened, and truth walked in? Well,
She thrived for a while by updating her devices,

Like — playing the metropolis, all the sleights of
Communications, the trick of the very new:
She was good at sudden taxis, away, in the small hours,
Had a dreadful skill with things like the letter
Never sent because of the promise to phone,
Never kept. And she had this vague gallery of

'Friends' to refer to, in a sensual, significant abstract,
No names vouchsafed. She was trying hard, was desperately
Applying the cosmetics of decline. — But she's
Abstract herself now; finally dead; not
Struck down by some other in contest, not replaced
By odder enchantments, not vanquished by any

Conversion from Snow Queens to Earth Mothers, none
Of that: she just couldn't keep up the pose.
It was not so long back that her last departure
Took place. She put out one entreating hand in velvet,
But it looked like something ghost-written for her.
I tried to feed those plaintive metaphors, I searched

The depths of my compassionate soul for faith
To keep her alive; but all the same she died.
And sad the way daylight lastly saw her sink,
Poor Mademoiselle Claudette: leaving shadows of stances only,
Vague rags of garments, tawdry stage properties,
And terribly dry pink tissues on bedroom floors.

Union Man

His liquid lunches will not have unhoned
This lean man, upright at the bar
With the minutes of the last executive
In a thick buff wallet, listening precisely
And working through strategies. His brow
Is furrowed with niceties, his craft
Is the unravelment and intertwining
Of clauses in tense agreements. He gives
A week-end course in grievance and recompense,
And Monday, drives via home to all his high
Cabinets of cases, when the telephone
Clangs to the carpet as he stretches out far to a file
On a distant shelf, and listening precisely.
In a city where minds are slabbed with gold,
He builds a sheltering-wall of brick; and how
The commonwealth doth need such justices.

Breach

Within a mile of a sea, which could be heard,
On a Chesterfield much too narrow,
On a night that was much too short,
These two achieved a rare sort of victory:

They carried through a completely unselfish,
Unkind-to-no-other-people act of love,
Between twelve twenty-seven and twelve
Forty-four, while the latest oil slick

Slurped at the sands in the dark.
Nightlong coastguards fought it with radioed
Data about its location, helicopters clattered
To neutralise the thing with chemical sprays,

And half the resort was out next morning, waiting
As for some dismal, predicted second coming.
But these two made their protest about
The general soilure of the world at the hands

Of the effortful and the crude by just one
Once-only, uncontrived breach
Of its chaos with love. And there should be
A plaque on the esplanade to this effect.

Ruse

Lastly my turn to hide, so
The other children instantly
Scattered among the scrubland grass,
Blanked their eyes, began
To count aloud.
         Away downhill,
The traffic thundered less
In the hazed streets, the orange
Street-lamps suddenly lit in
A necklace of twilight mauves. I was
Expected home from this game, to eat,
And read myself to sleep. Besides,
There were so many ruses more
I wanted to devise.
         Before
They counted out my time, came
Running to look for me, I ran
And left them there, I ran back home
And left them.
         Turning today
A tower-block corner, I saw them
In the gathering dark, bemused
And middle-aged, in tattered
Relics of children's clothes, still
Searching even now in the glittering
Scrubland of my Precinct, for
What had deserted them, what had
Cast them there; blank-eyed, and
Never to tell what I had built,
What I had left them with in forty years.

Holding Hands with Pregnant Women

Somewhere a bus drives on, on this chilling night
Of dusty April, between its termini,
The conductor winding his destinations
Backwards and forwards as if to obtain some
Renewal of the sense of quest; and these two
      Sit inside it all this time,

Holding hands and not noticing. She repeats,
'You would have wanted this child to be your own?'
And he gives her illusion no denial,
Having loved her enough, long since, to have felt
Exactly such a thing for about nine weeks
      When they met by the bandstand.

But truly he is thinking now, 'How can she
Be ever complete again, ever the same
As the woman of the past, when our pledges
Were engraved in deep letters and in our eyes
When we kissed by the boating-lake in the fog,
      And I could not bear to lose

The hand I capture now in this neutral way
Which *she* does not grasp?'
                  — But let them travel on.
Give or take a variation of detail,
It could be happening almost anywhere,
Wherever a woman gives a man her news
      And he makes out he is pleased,

Yet not for one moment wants her happiness,
Preferring a slow gathering of regret,
Of self-doubt about her marriage, and a fear
That she may have spoilt her life when, instead, she —
But pregnant today, she feels magnanimous
      Towards all unregenerate

Lovers arrived out of the past, who have lost
Their cutting edge of novelty or nuisance:
Those old, superannuated cavaliers
Who send birthday presents through friends' addresses
Or make phone calls to the office, gentle bores
      Who will always minister

To the last shards of romance, her tiny crave
For a tremor of nostalgia now and then.
There is this sweet island in her consciousness
Where the trees gleam even now with untaken
Fruit from those evenings on the rustic bridges
      Making quips about moorhens,

Having schemes about beds in far-off cities;
And even now, she thinks, he would if he could,
He would pluck it if she let him, and suck, suck;
So he holds her hand, in London or Belgrade,
Allowing these assumptions to have their rein
      — Yet wherever they may be,

He is looking for the sudden prize: the chance
To re-start the process all over again
With another one; at forty or fifty,
To begin a brand-new journey through it all,
All over again (the new girl saying how
      Alien it would be, in

Her married or unmarried state, to even
Dream of bearing children, how she quite intends
To stay sterile for her career, for the sake
Of peace and quiet, or fulfilment through batiks,
While she takes the pill, and smokes, and wonders if
      This Jungian analyst

Can put her together, and whether she should
Consent to be chairperson of her local
Liberal Women's Group). How he longs for it
All to flood back, that poignant high adventure
Of plunging into young women still unsoiled
        By cash and security . . .

He will therefore grip her patronising hand
Rather nominally, on whatever route
They ride today; and will outwardly maintain
A reverence for their past, and try to show
A nostalgia for it out of chivalry,
        As the unborn child begins

To chafe inside her. — And she would not believe
That last night's yearning for the larger size of
Gherkins, in big glossy jars, which you notice
On the counters of downmarket sidestreet pubs,
Was a throwback to their first drink ever, at
        The Hare and Hounds in Catford.

Find

The waxwork chef once gripped in two wax hands,
Grinning over it at his readers, a menu
In a square wooden frame. The frame is empty,
And the chef lies grinning on his side in an overlooked yard
Behind a washeteria; presenting his lack of choice
To the gush of a drainpipe.
                           When they learn
The value of this site, and finally all
The bulldozed earth clumps down on him, he will make
A find for a commercial archaeologist: he will mean
Someone's failure to make it in this world.
He did not work. He does not work tonight,
In the little darkening yard.
                           So call it flesh
To ashes, and wax to wax: in the crumbling
Sewers of the city the waters are rising, the eating
Is going on in another, lighted place.
On this raining night, successful faces elsewhere
Shine out like artifacts of burnished wax.
                           They read,
Through their private spectacle-frames, what wine
Might gush from the list held out by the living hands.

On the Day

He thanks whoever-she-is for her thoughtful
Beneficence to him, in that visitation
In the early hours of the morning on the day
He travels up to hear what the X-ray meant:
Appearing out of a carmine snowdrift and
Lustrously uncovering; then extending
Such long quick legs around him, and pushing
Him widely awake to smile at the dawn for once.

If he remembers ruefully that no one now
Visits of their own free will, that you visit
All your dreams on yourself, still, either way,
His world comes right for a while. In the lift,
As it drops to the snowing street, he knows
That either some she, or some part of himself,
Wants to will him even yet into life again
— Something is pushing schemes for winning time.

A View of Sussex

Our happy road is flanked by russet guards-
Of-honour, for November: tiny leaves
Flit at our wheels in suicidal pairs
As we drive powerfully south. You shake your head
Because you want to rearrange the hair
You won't let anybody see you comb
Except yourself. — And there, see how the lamp
Lights up those gables where the vine has turned
A dry vermilion round the 'Hawk and Prey',
Which flaps and creaks for the wind. We smell of air
As I grip hard on our receptionist's
Black ballpen, and write lies. But further in,
Along the corridors, the mantle of
The central heat comes down, a thrilling hush
Which deepens in our room. We drop our bags
Hard on a bench of wooden slats, we let
The tap drip and the light stay on, we start
Clutching the white stiff sheets to tear them back
As if we were ravening at new bread.

Ceremony

The Old Fox glimpses the little bag passing
Furtively round. They are secretly
Collecting for him in the office, he is going to retire.

The little bag, something tells him, will be light;
Not with an excess of paper money either.
The Old Fox is not popular where he works.
The typists have given 2p, the Under Manager
Ten, the Manager puts in a fifty
And takes out thirty-eight.
. . . It might not reach two pounds.

For forty-three years' service, two pounds or less!
The Old Fox cogitates quietly at his desk
(So quietly not even his secretary divines
He is cogitating at all).
Well, he could act the martyr, he could break down and weep
In front of the whole staff at his presentation.
He could make an acerbic speech and scathe the lot.

He could, out of humility, refuse
To have them make such a fuss of him: 'Forty-three
Years in so happy a firm seems not so long.'
But he has another idea.

The Old Fox knows where they keep
The key of the cupboard where the little bag
Is hidden in a teapot at night.
                                    The evening before,
On a pretence of tidying up loose ends,
He stays altruistically late, the last to leave,
He fetches the key, he opens the cupboard,

He takes out the bag,
And he puts in the sixteen five pound notes he has drawn in
                                        the lunch hour
Through the youngest clerk in the bank.

At his presentation next day, the Old Fox
Breaks down and gratefully weeps in front of the whole staff.

Procedural

The Old Fox sits at the front in the Chairman's eye, he
Questions the Apologies for Absence, he
Questions the Minutes, including
The accuracy of the amendments in these Minutes
To the Minutes of the meeting before last, he
Raises Matters Arising for half an hour.

Then he
Carps at the order of items on the Agenda,
Queries the omission of items *from* the Agenda,
Interrupts, interjects, raises Points of Information,
Asks innocent (loaded) questions, has serious Points of Order,
Puts down motions, puts down amendments to motions,
Puts down amendments to amendments, questions the voting,
Wants the Chairman to state again exactly what it is
They have decided by the voting,
Wants his disagreement with the Chairman's decision minuted,
Quotes the Constitution,
Waves the Companies Act.

The Old Fox proposes the creation of
Sub-committees, steering committees, working parties and
Working groups, and declines election
To any of them himself. Any Other Business
Is devoted to matters raised by the Old Fox alone.

When the time to decide the Date of Next Meeting arrives, he
Objects on sound grounds to every possible date.
The desk diaries wearily rise from dispatch cases once again,
The overcoats stay unbuttoned, the great white pages

Turn and flutter and the flutter becomes a wind
And the wind becomes a gale tearing
At the darkness outside the window,
At the darkness in everybody's soul in the steamed-up room.

When the storm subsides, the Old Fox
Has disappeared until the next time.

The Seventh Knight and the Green Cat:
A Variation on the Gawain Poet

Curious about her seven daughters, in turn came
The seven fortitudinous knights. And the first
To sit by the swarming fire, sipping mead with
Mother and eldest daughter, saw with much delight
The white cat pace to him, as he loved them,
Cats.
       The creature was unbleached to a queer
Shifting shade of green by the colours of the room
— Green hangings, green velvet on the couches,
Green branches at the window, green eyes in matron and girl,
Green even in the flames of the fire because
They cast salt in the crevices of the coals to
Make matching colours.
           So the white cat
Mewed at him, nudged his ankle, mounted his lap,
And the mother murmured, 'You are honoured, she
Has never before walked in such a way up to a man.'

This flattery went deep, proposals were made, and the pair
Duly wed.
       And since daughters must dutifully marry,
And mothers must needs be mothers, and marry off,
A second knight came seeking the second daughter
And chose a green chair by the great fire while
The mother poured wine.
          And willingly again the white
Cat rose on her green cushion, stood stretching,
And pattered the flagstones to the handsome second knight
To form fond figures-of-eight round the man's thin legs.
'There's a something about you that attracts her, she
Has never lingered with a man,' the lady said;
And in this style was her second daughter secured
To a cat-adoring knight.
         This way it went too
With the third, the fourth, the fifth and the sixth, on

A succession of green days with the cat casually
Trusting its truly-said-to-be-so-untypical
Affection to the different knights, whether of
Transylvania, Tartary, Aragon or Tibet, being
Similar only in their peculiar pride at pre-empting,
Uniquely, an unsociable animal unsure of men:
Cat-lovers, but gullible with it, which is rare.

On the last and greenest day, green curtains gathering
Across the storm which sent green branches seething
Over the sky in a frenzied trellis-work of green,
The seventh knight finally knocked; one who knew
And loved cats more than any of these lovers, and
He yearned for the youngest daughter's hand.

                                      Her mother
Decanted liquor as usual, and the lovely daughter sat,
And green flames flashed in the hearth as the cat
Began again, greenly, its meaningful trek of the floor.
'She will not go to you, she has never yet greeted a man,'
The matron predicted; but the cat pounced all at once,
From no definable angle, onto the very codpiece of the doting
Knight, and neatly nestled.

                       So the mother and girl
Cried equally with eagerness and ecstasy as before

— At which this knight bounded up from his bench of green,
Shouting, 'I am getting out of here at once!'
And 'I know what sort of a situation this is,'
Dropping the cat, flat-eared and snarling with dire dismay,
And decapitating the thing with a dirk;
With screams from all, except himself and the evil cat's
Head, which jeered, and rejoined itself to the body
And said, 'What was that intended to imply?'
'The true friend of cats,' said the knight, 'knows
That cat in ninety-nine which walks for women
And not for itself alone, the animal which is
The familiar of witches.

                    But it seems as if
I did not exorcise this one quite enough.'

'You are remarkably right,' said the reconstituted cat
Sapiently, 'and for this wisdom you will wend,
By a promise you will here and now provide,
One year through numerous travails of the world, and come
To the terrible temple of the cat-goddess,
Mere pictures of whom inflict fevers and death on
Temerarious beholders who brave them, and
Leading lady of many a savage psychotropic
Trance. There we shall truly meet again,
And I shall take my turn.'

                              So the seventh knight
Ground on grimly over the bogs and crags of the world,
Lodging roughly, going rudely his slow way
On a bewildered horse through innumerable bleak,
Colourless, sleazy, subtopiate regions,
Demoralizing tracts of megalosuburbia,
And came, just after eleven heavy months, to a splendid
Castle, where his welcome was very grand.
                                        And there,
In the course of prattle at dinner about property prices,
He thought he might try to elicit where the temple
Of the great cat-goddess stood, half-hoping it had not
Survived redevelopment.
                        'My fine fellow, I can
Tell you the lie of the land,' said the lord his host,
'But linger a little while here, enjoy some relaxation'
— And his lady smiled in sly sympathy and accord —
'While I do some terribly tiresome hunting. And, by the way,
Be good!'
          With a feeling of distant *déjà vu*,
The seventh knight agreed; and for three successive days,
Was allowed to lie lazily in his bed while his host
Went hunting and left his lady (just as he had read);
Because, in short, truncating a tangled tale,
Coming in sleek, scarlet, delightful garments,
She insisted on sleeping with him thoroughly each of the three
Days her husband was happily hunting the evening meal,

Which the knight agreed to with an anxious sense of
Compromise; and suspicion.
                         Each night, the master,
Hot and bothered and scenting himself, brought back
The special spoils of a strenuous day in the field;
For this supper asking nothing in return and reward
But the knight's good company in anecdote and carousing;
And on the last day, as promised, he provided
Instructions for reaching the great cat-goddess's place.

It proved a daunting plod over muddy areas,
An extremely unclean excursion, so that when the knight
Arrived there, both he and his horse exhausted,
Spattered in the saddle from travel, he thought it was his
                                       tiredness
That stopped him from seeing where it was. But suddenly,
He saw it: a low, brick thing nearly hidden in the grasses
Of a thistly field, with peculiar peep-holes from which
Any occupant, sitting safely in a nook, could
Scan out.
                Dismounting, the knight called, clearly, and as
Loudly as he was able, on whoever lurked inside to
Emerge; and there expeditiously appeared a
Truly tremendous cat, the size of a full-grown woman.
'As I promised and pledged I would do, in all duty,'
Stated the knight, 'I have travelled to the temple
Of the great cat-goddess, to pay the penalty for
Following up certain suspicions too rashly,
And acting in anger.'
                  Then the cat mysteriously smiled,
Saying, 'Listen. As an artful knight, you showed
Some shrewdness in discerning a witch's cat;
As a truly brave one you moved boldly
Against a defenceless, domestic beast; as
A plodder you showed profound persistence
In going your way through the world for a year
To find out this frightful place; as a seizer of chances,
You lay three times with the lady of the castle,

Obviously not having offered any oath you would thereby
Break; thus an immaculate code of knightly
Tactics you have most tightly kept, and
Will be rightly rewarded.'
                            At which the vast animal
Cast off its outer cat-costume and calmly stepped forth
As the seventh daughter, dressed in the delightful,
Scarlet, sleek garments of the mistress of the castle.

'I was,' she said, 'all the time secretly concealed
In the little anatomy of the cat, and in the body
Of the lady of the castle you came to know a bit,
And the knight of the castle, my loving master and lord,
Was all the time my own dear mother in drag.
So on the basis of all that, you may bow and beg now
The hand of the youngest daughter you came to collect.
There is no way out.'
                            So, haltingly heeding
These dreadful words, the dumbstruck fellow put
His proposals, too perplexed to do other, and the pair
Were rapidly wed.
                            And they went on to work through
Many years of irrefrangible, retributive wedlock
(For the daughter turned out termagant as well as witch);
But concerning these travails I cannot truthfully say
I am sad or sorry, and cannot make this knight seem
An object of proper pity: as a grown-up, I regard
Knights and knighthood and the mores and weapons
Of a warrior society as both juvenile and degrading.